HOW LONG

How Long

BY RON PADGETT

COFFEE HOUSE PRESS

MINNEAPOLIS 2011

Coffee House Press books are available to the trade through our primary distributor, Consortium Book Sales & Distribution, www.cbsd.com or (800) 283-3572. For personal orders, catalogs, or other information, write to: info@coffeehousepress.org.

Coffee House Press is a nonprofit literary publishing house. Support from private foundations, corporate giving programs, government programs, and generous individuals helps make the publication of our books possible. We gratefully acknowledge their support in detail in the back of this book. To you and our many readers around the world, we send our thanks for your continuing support.

Good books are brewing at coffeehousepress.org

LIBRARY OF CONGRESS CATALOGING-IN-PUBLICATION DATA
Padgett, Ron, 1942–
How long / by Ron Padgett.
p. cm.
ISBN 978-1-56689-256-8 (alk. paper)
I. Title.
ps3566.a32h57 2011
811'.54—dc22
2010038005

ACKNOWLEDGMENTS
Some of these poems appeared, sometimes in different versions, in *Aphros*, *Columbia Poetry Review*, *Court Green*, *Denver Quarterly*, *The Poetry Project Newsletter*, *The Recluse*, *Shampoo*, and *Zoland Poetry*, and on the website of the Academy of American Poets.

"Anniversary Waltz" was published as a broadside, designed by Clifton Meador and printed by April Sheridan at the Center for Book and Paper Arts, Columbia College Chicago.

"From Dante" appeared as a chapbook, designed and printed by Colin Frazer at The Press at Colorado College.

"I'll Get Back to You" was included in a catalogue for an exhibition by Barney Kulok.

"Urn Burial," "How Long," and "What Are You On?" were included in Jim Dine's book series, *Hot Dreams*.

"The Song of René Descartes" appeared as a booklet, designed and printed by Jacky Essirard at the Ateliér de Villemorge, Angers (France).

For George

Contents

Scotch Tape Body

I never thought,
forty years ago,
taping my poems into a notebook,
that one day the tape
would turn yellow, grow brittle, and fall off
and that I'd find myself on hands and knees
groaning as I picked the pieces up
off the floor
one by one

Of course no one thinks ahead like that
If I had
I would have used archival paste
or better yet
not have written those poems at all

But then I wouldn't have had
the pleasure of reading them again,
the pleasure of wincing
and then forgiving myself,
of catching glimpses of who I was
and who I thought I was,
the pleasure—is that the word?—of seeing
that that kid really did exist.

The Death Deal

Ever since that moment
when it first occurred
to me that I would die
(like everyone on earth!)
I struggled against
this eventuality, but
never thought of
how I'd die, exactly,
until around thirty
I made a mental list:
hit by car, shot
in head by random ricochet,
crushed beneath boulder,
victim of gas explosion,
head banged hard
in fall from ladder,
vaporized in plane crash,
dwindling away with cancer,
and so on. I tried to think
of which I'd take
if given the choice,
and came up time
and again with He died
in his sleep.
Now that I'm offcially old,

2

though deep inside not
old offcially or otherwise,
I'm oddly almost cheered
by the thought
that I might find out
in the not too distant future.
Now for lunch.

Grasshopper

It's funny when the mind thinks about the psyche,
as if a grasshopper could ponder a helicopter.

It's a bad idea to fall asleep
while flying a helicopter:

when you wake up, the helicopter is gone
and you are too, left behind in a dream,

and there is no way to catch up,
for catching up doesn't figure

in the scheme of things. You are
who you are, right now,

and the mind is so scared it closes its eyes
and then forgets it has eyes

and the grasshopper, the one that thinks
you're a helicopter, leaps onto your back!

He is a brave little grasshopper
and he never sleeps

for the poem he writes is the act
of always being awake, better than anything

you could ever write or do.
Then he springs away.

Kit

Tamburlaine crashed through
around 1375. Marlowe
had written his play by 1587.
The intervening years bled
into history, the fourteenth
a very bloody century.
Good that Marlowe waited
to be born suffciently later,
thus avoiding the real
Tamburlaine, who might have
torn his head off.
But he died young anyway,
did Marlowe, not even thirty.
The "high astounding terms"
he promised he delivered.
Still it makes me mad
that he got stabbed to death,
though I have to admit
it's part of his appeal.

The Curvature of Royalty

One of the surprising things about modern life
is that quite a few countries still have kings and queens
and palaces for them to live in
as well as great wealth to use or even have!
These kings and queens accept the idea
that they should be kings and queens,
just as many people born to money
accept their wealth as natural
and most poor people assume
that poverty is their destiny
no matter what they say to the contrary.
Everything points toward Fate:
the rocks are as they are, the clouds too, the giraffe
and the cantaloupe are all lined up
facing an imaginary point of origin
like lines in a diagram of perspective,
and though the lines bend slightly through time
everyone bends with them, so the dung beetle
remains a figure of comedy.
Further along the chain of evolution
he becomes the court jester
juggling words and jumping around
in the debris of falling syntax.
The King laughs mightily, the Queen quietly,
for though they have become playing cards

they still can be amused,
and at any moment they can roll off the cards
and onto the floor of their palace
where they can laugh all they want
and the servants will keep looking straight ahead.

Urn Burial

Sir Thomas Browne said
that it is useless to erect monuments
in the hope of being remembered
by generations far into the future
since the future itself
will cease to exist. That is,
the world would be destroyed soon,
hence "'Tis too late to be ambitious."
Apparently this belief was widely held
by English people in the seventeenth century.
My grandmother, in the twentieth century,
took a curious pleasure in pursing her lips and stating
"The Bible says the world will last
one thousand years but not two," which meant that I
could not live past the age of 58
and might be there for The End of the World.
Fortunately I did not believe her
and unfortunately it made me think
she was a little bit crazy and certainly thoughtless
in saying such a thing to her young grandson.
The Bible also says that Methuselah
lived to the age of 969. They should have chosen
a more credible number, for, as Joe Brainard asked,
"If a hundred-year-old man can barely stand up,
can you imagine what it would be like to be five hundred?"

I can barely imagine what it is like to be *any* age,
though I can imagine what it is like to be dead
because I have woken up after a deep sleep
with no memory of it.
So you don't have to imagine anything
to know what being dead is like.
One less thing to worry about!
Unless, of course, I'm wrong about the afterlife,
and fiery demons prod you with red-hot tridents
into the writhing maw of an inferno of glistening snakes.
Fortunately this happens only to Christians—
fortunately for me, that is.
Sir Thomas Browne was a Christian
but I hope he believed he'd go to Paradise,
for it seems too bad such a wise and learnèd man
should think that he would go to Hell.
Browne lived to 77, to the day.
I'm not sure the exactitude means anything here,
but for his time he was quite old,
and possibly surprised to wake up and find himself
892 years younger than Methuselah, or wake up
and find himself at all, in bed, and still on earth!
Then he died.
"I didn't plan on living this long,"
said my other grandmother, at 96,
"but I just keep on breathing."

We Three Kings

We three kings of Orient
are

disoriented.

We came all this way
only to get lost?

"Get lost!" is what
they said

when we said
"Are we here?"

Now we are really lost
and disillusioned too.

It's true
our cigars were loaded

on the backs of imaginary camels

but we thought the world
could use a good laugh.

I guess we were wrong.

Death

Let's change the subject.
In the hills an occasional noise—
shotgun here, bloodcurdling shriek there, hey
nonny nonny, and two boys,
lost, weird, homeless, starving, about to be
eaten by a big black bear! O muse avert thine eyes!
(I will look *for* you.)
             The bear shambles forth
on his hind legs, so shaggy they are
and smelly, and waves his forepaws in the air as if
he were erasing the blackboard on which
our fate is written, and the boys have hair
standing up on their heads and the trees lean back
as far as trees can lean and not fall down, they
hate that hair! I do too! (Muse, don't look yet.)

But then a man comes through the woods
with comb and scissors—it's barber Tom, come
to give those boys a haircut and the bear one too,
if it wants, and it does, and all three share
in this tonsorial moment, hair
falling softly on the forest floor.

Walking with Walt

When everyday objects and tasks
seem to crowd into the history you live in
you can't breathe so easily you can hardly breathe at all
the space is so used up,
when yesterday there was nothing but.
Ah, expansive America! you
must have existed. Otherwise
no Whitman.

It's funny that America did not explode
when Whitman published *Leaves of Grass,*
explode with amazement and pride, but
America was busy being other
than what he thought it was and I grew up
thinking along his lines and of course now
oh well

though actually at this very moment
the trees are acting exactly the way they did
when he walked through and among them,
one of the roughs, as he put it,
though how rough I don't know I think
he was just carried away

as we all are, if we're lucky
enough to have just walking
buoy us up a little off the earth
to be more on it

Inaction of Shoes

There are many things to be done today
and it's a lovely day to do them in

Each thing a joy to do
and a joy to have done

I can tell because of the calm I feel
when I think about doing them

I can almost hear them say to me
Thank you for doing us

And when evening comes
I'll remove my shoes and place them on the floor

And think how good they look
sitting? . . . standing? . . . there

Not doing anything

The Center of Gravity

The military Jeep was said
to have had a high center
of gravity, therefore
subject to tipping:
if you took a curve too fast
you might turn over.
A person with very short legs
has a low center of gravity
and will not tip over easily.
The ottoman likewise.
When a person is lying flat
he or she has the lowest center
of gravity possible, as does
a sheet of paper on a table.
People floating around
in outer space have little
or no center of gravity
because there's not enough gravity
to have a center.
Gravidanza is the Italian word
for pregnancy, which sounds
more serious than the English word
and may remind us of sentences such as
"The situation is very grave."
Every situation has gravity,

it's a question of how much.
People too have gravity—
of manner, of morals, and of body.
It is good to have gravity
but not too much of it:
like a bag of cement,
you might not be able to move
around or make ethical distinctions.
But with too little of it
you are flighty, your feet
hardly touch the ground.
Though cement and flightiness
have their charms,
it's better to find
your center of gravity
and have it be the place
you radiate out from.

Once I lay in bed ill, unable to move,
but in my head
I was flying and bouncing around.
But illness has no charm
and when it becomes very grave
your gravity edges toward
the most perfect center of gravity ever.

Earl Grey

That cup of Earl Grey
didn't perk me up.
What time is dinner?
It is approaching at the rate
of time, that is, one second per second.
I hear kitchen clangs and thumps.
What a joy to sit here and think
of oven mitts!
But what about Earl Grey, he
of the beautiful name?
What if Earl was not his name,
but a title, like *Baron* Munchausen
or *Count* Dracula?
The aristocracy is hard to understand,
its ranks and privileges and its nuances,
just as military ranks don't mean much
unless you're a Rear Vice-Admiral:
you know exactly who and what you are.
And here I am, a drowsy, happy bum.

Material World

Letting it stream in the light and air
and wanting it to and having it in the room next to you
as if a person made of light and air
could materialize here

I and everyone else
have materialized

Karl Marx
based his ideas
on materialism

and if you look at his face and beard
you cannot see a single ray of light
and you cannot imagine that he breathed air

Karl Marx
Ar ar

The pine tree, the fir, the larch
high in the cool morning

It is hard to say how far more important
trees are than Karl Marx

At the age of three Marx did not say
I wish I were a tree
and of course the tree is always saying
No comment

even though you are dancing with that tree
while overhead a small Greek deity
is circling on a glissando we call wings
on the verge of materialization
and here we are

What Are You On?

If you asked an Elizabethan
What are you on?
he or she would have answered
The earth, this terrestrial globe
whereas today it means
What medication
are you taking?
(Are you taking has less energy
than *What medication* it is an anticlimax
without a climax)
And today *What are you on about?*
would have sounded like
What are you of thereabouts in?
and will
So what medications *are*
you on?
I am taking italics it pokes
a hole in whatever is going to be
so I can slip through
and not have arms and legs all the time
You've lost me and I'm not even an Elizabethan
That's O.K. neither am I though both
of us bestride this terrestrial globe
and fain would lie down
for the earth is a medication a giant pill

we ride on
like the aspirin in the poem I wrote in 1966
and didn't understand until last night or was it this morning
A.M. and P.M. are medications
I take one in the morning and one in the evening

Some day people will look back
at the twentieth century and think
How backward they were
the way some look back now
at tribal societies and say
But primitive life was so dirty how
could you keep things clean?
not knowing that tribal people
lived in the Garden of Eden
comparatively speaking
That is they had more humanity
than later people
who traded theirs for technology
so that those people who look back at Earth
some day from a distant galaxy
will not be people at all
comparatively speaking
they will be cue balls

But this morning I am not in a billiard situation the sun
is shining onto my house and the trees
are feeling like their tops because they are still in the Garden of Eden

that is the gentle endless hush
of an endless mother to her endless newborn child
Things are there
covered with sparkles
that have nothing to do with sunlight
the way one night I got out of bed and found
that I was covered with sparkles very small ones
I wondered if I would be covered with sparkles the rest of my life
and if other people had them
But these are not the same sparkles that things have on them
except the ocean sometimes at night

By day the ocean moves away from where it was
but a mountain does not
Somewhere in between lies Hidden Valley
where Grandpa comes out of his cabin
and staggers around the dooryard
then goes back inside
where Grandma is holding a baking tin
of fresh hot biscuits
but she will give him none
Give me some biscuits he cries
but she smiles and shakes her head
They are all for me she exults
and then laughs she is only joking
Grandpa sits down at the table
and pretends to be dead
revived only by the muffled thud of the biscuit tin

Where's mah coffee he roars
even though he sees it in the cup before him
and Grandma says We're plumb out
That's how the day begins in Hidden Valley

But where are the grandchildren
They are scattered about the world in jagged pieces
that move like birds in spring
with colors and speedometers on them
Someday they will return to Hidden Valley
and form another mountain
to make Hidden Valley even more hidden
when the waterfall closes over it

You think I don't know where it is

or is that just a ploy to get me to tell you?
You are like the guy who looked all over
for his hat and later learned it was on his head
but it didn't mean anything until he realized he had a head
and that the hat was both on and inside it
and when he did
it was not a rabbit that he pulled out
but a rectangle in which the rabbit was imprisoned
You don't want to be that guy, do you?
You would rather be the rabbit
when all along you could have been the waterfall

We move ahead in our story to five years later
then we move five years back
because there is no story
only a collection of events with no beginning,
no end, and therefore no middle, it is all
one big beginning, middle, and end every second
and though you are in it you are also to the side
like an actor waiting in the wings for the cue
that will cause the stage to light up and expand
though it is also the cue for the audience to rise
and head for the exits, because *they* are the real players
and you, it turns out, are part of the scenery
propped up against a wall, gathering dust along your top ridge,
for soon you will be transported to Hidden Valley
and placed among the other mountains

One of these mountains is the Earl of Essex
covered with the crud
of having galloped all the way across Wales and England nonstop
Essex who dashed up the palace stairs and barged
into Elizabeth's private chamber unannounced
—where no man had ever set foot—
midst the gasps and cries of her ladies-in-waiting
and there it is
his face
on the front of his head
and her face coming off her head
and starting toward him

because she knew right then his head
would be severed from his body
but what she did not know
is that he too would end up in Hidden Valley
raining down his sparkles upon the house of Grandma and Grandpa

Are you enjoying your vacation
Yes I am
in fact so much that I don't even think of it as a vacation or as
    anything else
and come to think of it I don't even think of it
it's just the way things are
How about you
Yes I too am enjoying my vacation
Well good

Silence

What you just said about your vacation I'm not sure I understand
    what you mean
I didn't mean much of anything I guess
The mountains around here have a way of making me not think very
    much
maybe because they aren't thinking at all who knows
and I tend to become like whatever I'm around

But you're always around air do you turn into air
Yes I'm always air

What about Grandma and Grandpa are you turning into them
No I can't turn into them I already *am* them

Well that is very interesting
but I have to scoot along now

And a fine day to you as well

Ireland rose up on the horizon
backlit by history
but Hidden Valley was too powerful it made Ireland sink back down
though the voices of Ireland could be heard in the distance
some singing others laughing and some wailing and scolding
and then they too faded when Grandpa brandished his lips at them

for he wished to sing himself
and all alone on the veranda of his own personality
the one built partly by him and partly by the celestial carpenters
who found his scratchy gurgling caterwauling arias to be as
    astonishing
as he found them to be beautiful and moving—
arias that caused tears to gush forth from the sky
you could see when you looked up into his eyes
not long after you were born
the sky at night

and professional wrestling was on TV
Antonino Rocca bounded around the ring

evading horrible huge guys who fought dirty

the kind you would find only in New York City

when it was in black and white

little Antonino who looked like a short-order cook in a diner

but who dodged and slid and leaped so fast

the horrible big guys couldn't catch him

but when they did, Ow! Get away, Antonino!

and he came back to life and slithered free

and hurled the big guys down and one-two-three boom

they were pinned

and once more he smiled

at people like us out in the middle of nowhere

prompting Grandpa to clear his throat and say

It's time for bed it's way past time

and it was

but we were hidden outside of time

and no one would know

because they were visible inside of time

I was happy in Hidden Valley happy enough

and I'm happy I once lived there

Maybe I'll find myself there again someday

even though the mountains will be gone

and the rest changed beyond all recognition

The Hatchet Man

God
give me the strength
to raise this hatchet
over my head
and strike
with all my force
the cubic foot of air
that I imagine
to be in front of me
one foot off the floor
and to strike it so
as to cleave it right in half
and watch the two halves fall
to the left and to the right
still one foot
above the floor

But God did not
answer my prayer
and I remain here
with the hatchet

The cube
is not here

It went away
and took God
with it
and he doesn't have
a hatchet

What a funny life he leads!

Spots

And so once again
Father Time said to Mother Nature,
"Mother, put a few more of those brown spots
on him, please," and so she did,
dutifully and without malice she placed them
here and there
among the others she had left before
as gentle reminders, though if
you've ever looked in the mirror
and noticed several that weren't there
the night before . . . I lose
my train of thought, it was on Herrengracht
the cobblestones were irregular
for pedestrian feet such as mine
so I kept looking down when I most wanted
to look straight ahead and around.
"The Earth is a cobblestone,"
said Father Time to Mother Nature,
but she made no reply
for she did not like fancy allusions
to her cousin Mother Earth.
The kitchen became edgy
for a moment and then it passed,
the edginess, that is,
along with the moment: both

were moved along to the area
of Past Experiences and from there
shunted into The Forgotten.

But I remembered it was my birthday
and my mother is large with me
and her mind is full of ironing
like music you can't stop hearing in your head,
the music of ironing, and so
me, first a spot, then a boy
with a dog named Spot,
and now a man on whom more spots
are arriving in the night,
when Mother Nature makes her rounds
and Father Time keeps the watch.

Happy Birthday to Us

for Marcello Padgett

Seeing as it
is my birthday
I thought
I'd say something
cheerful
and true:
first thing
this morning
my grandson,
age now
90 days,
gave me smile
after smile
and I gave him one
for every one
he gave me.
That it's the ninth
straight day
of rain
doesn't matter
one whit
because
I've always felt
that June 17

is a special day,
a sunny,
blessèd day
I was lucky
to be born
on. And here
I am, a lucky
dog whose bark
means he's glad
you've come.
It's your birthday
too, Marcello,
because I give it
to you. Now
you have two.
I don't
really need
one anymore.

On Decency

Practicing decency
is easier when you are surrounded
by cannibals who are nice to you,
nice because they are line drawings of cannibals
and you are a cannibal also
though a real one.
But when you are not a cannibal
and you are among sheep and clothespins,
no, not clothespins, those are the fingers
of those who are pinching the sheep
to keep them awake in midair,
then it is much harder
and at times seemingly pointless,
like a cement philosophy
that dead-ends on both ends.

Thus we took leave of the city
where our five senses had been compressed
into a shiny black ball rolling always just ahead of us
along with the pink ball of our mortality
and the white ball of our idea of ourselves,
as if we were moving along on the baize
of a huge billiard table.

In 1942
I took leave of my senses

and became a person
and a stone and an oaf,
but deep in my little human heart
I wanted decency,
for the tree, for all of you, and for part of me
(the oaf).
I pulled myself up through time
against the undertow of my oafishness,
as if I were holding my breath
until the day when decency would be everywhere
the way everywhere already was,
but each time I opened my eyes
the decency fled—
I saw its coattails rounding a corner
just like that.

Mother, you had decency, certainly, and father,
you did too, though sometimes it was hidden
among the smoking fragments that fly up
into heaven behind Zeus as he ascends,
and you, Grandma and Grandpa, and Grandma,
you all had decency, you always had it,
fresh off the land that has no malice in it.
I had no land, but I had you.

Irish Song by an English Man

O there's a listening in the air
There's a hovering nearby
I know because I'm there
And it is I

O there's a mountain in the stream
All to ribbons torn
Almost a dream
The moment you are born

O my mother came to me
Without a reason why
I wanted to be free
Of her and die

I loved her like a harp
Whose strings have gone away
To ripple in the dark
No songs anyway

Except O the one I hear
And no one hears but I
A listening in the air
A hovering nearby

I'll Get Back to You

What was I thinking about
a few minutes ago when
another thought
swept me away?
Can't I have (pepper)
several thoughts at the same time
(carnival midway) or go back and forth
between (hyphen) them?
I guess so!
But since people (ooga) don't
like that kind of thinking (factory)
we don't do it (doghouse) much.
I never wanted to live (tree)
in a doghouse.
Now to get back (folding
map) to that earlier thought.
(President is guarding it.)
(No sense in asking *him* for it.)
It had something to do
with numbers (flying up
all over the place) and how
(smoke) sequence has properties
that (gleaming faucets) induce
certain thoughts and feelings,
such as reassurance.

I guess that's a good argument
for linearity. Don't you prefer
linearity in the long run?
(Low clouds over the winter field.)

Thinking about a Cloud

There's not a lot of time to think
when one is assailed by activities and obligations
and even less time to do it
when one is free of them
because then one spends one's time thinking
about how little time there is.

That's what it's like to be in America
early in the twenty-first century:
there are fewer spaces left
between things, and it is in these spaces
that thought comes forth
and walks around and lies down
sometimes all at the same time
it is so elastic and like an altocumulus cloud
with a sense of humor.
Hello, cloud. It's nice to see you again.
It says, "A cloud does not reply, it *is* a reply."
"But you just answered me."
"No, that was you answering yourself."
"But you enabled me to do so, didn't you?"
"Yes, but only because you believed it possible."
"Are you implying that anything I believe possible will happen?"
"No, I never imply anything. In fact I never say anything."
"Oh, I forgot. It's just that

it's hard for me to talk with you, knowing you don't talk."

"What makes you think that it matters?"

"I don't know. Perhaps my belief

  that we may as well think that it matters,

  for otherwise we would sit down and turn into a puddle."

"You are the first person ever to use the word *puddle* in a poem," said the

    cloud. "Please don't do it again."

"I was thinking of you, how high up you are,

  and yet sometimes even you become a puddle."

"I never become anything. You forget: I am not a cloud."

"I forgot because I thought you might go away

  before I had a chance to talk with you."

"Well, you've had your chance, and perhaps you will have others later,

  but for now, even as I speak, you feel me slipping away."

"Yes, I do, it's like knowing something terrible, little by little."

"Don't use the word *little* so much, either. You're a grown-up now."

"Are there grown-up clouds too? You sound like one."

"I sound like one because I am almost gone.

  And when I am gone, you will hear

  only the sound of your own personality

  as it rises in you and pushes me away.

  Don't you hear it now?"

Crush

Or heck
why not just, just
go over and tell her
how you feel,
you have a temperature
of 98.6 degrees F.
and a pulse rate of
175 and blood
pressure at whoosh
whoosh whoosh oh way
too high the cuff
is going to explode!
—or get up and go
home and cry your
heart out and be
a hopeless wimp
for all I care.

I Remember Lost Things

I remember getting letters addressed to me with my name and
street address, followed on the next line by the word *City*. Which
meant the same city in which they had been mailed. Could life
have been that simple?

I remember the first time I heard Joe read from his *I Remember*.
The shock of pleasure was quickly replaced by envy and the
question, Why didn't I think of that? Aesthetic pleasure comes
in many forms and degrees, but envy comes only when you
wholeheartedly admire someone else's new work. Envying
the talent of a person you love is particularly beautiful and
envigorating. And you don't even have to answer the question.

I remember feeling miffed at García Lorca because he made
me feel like crying about something that may never have
happened. There is a 1929 photograph of him standing next to
a large sphere on a granite pedestal that also bears a sundial,
on the Columbia University campus. Passing by the sundial
this morning, I suddenly realized that Lorca had stood on that
very spot 70 years ago, a few years before he was shot to death.
It was as if he had been there just moments ago. Such a brutal,
stupid death! Tears came to my eyes. But on second thought,
I found it hard to believe that someone would put such a large
sphere on this spot: it would have come between the light and
the sundial, no? Later, when I examined the photo again, I saw

that it *was* taken there. But that sphere? I like it because it keeps distracting me from the idea of his death.

I remember the mill, a piece of currency that was used for a few years near the end of World War II and just after. A thick paper (and later a lightweight metal) coin with a round hole in the center, the mill was worth one-tenth of a cent. It was fun to press it hard enough between thumb and forefinger to create temporary bumps on those fingers. On price tags, it was written as if it were an exponent; for example, ten cents and four mills was written 10^4. I don't know if mills were used anywhere other than in my hometown, and since they went out of use I have heard references to them only once or twice. They have faded away, even more forgotten than the black pennies of the same period. But if you mention the mill to people old enough to remember them, their faces will take on a rising glow of recognition that turns into a deeper pleasure in your company.

I am trying to remember what it felt like to have never even heard of television, to be six years old with your toys and maybe a dog. You roll the wooden truck along the carpet and make a truck sound that turns into a honking horn as you approach the outstretched paw of the dog that jumps to her feet, just in case, and you say, "Aw, I wouldn't have hit you." Wagging her tail, she comes up to lick your face, which is fun at first, before the doggy breath becomes too strong. Then you wipe your face with your sleeve, turn back to the truck, and start up its engine again. The sound of dishes from the kitchen.

I remember when some cars, older ones, had running boards, and the fun of standing on one and gripping the window post as the car accelerated down the block to the corner, the wind in my ears. Gradually there were fewer and fewer of them, and then none. At least the new cars still had hood ornaments, the most memorable being the shiny chrome head of an Indian man, his profile knifing into the wind, headdress feathers blown back. And then he was gone too.

The Apples in Chandler's Valley

The apples are red again in Chandler's Valley
— Kenneth Patchen

I figured that Chandler's Valley was a real place
but I didn't need to know where,
it was just some place with apple trees,
in America, of course,
but when it went on
"redder for what happened there"
a chill went up my spine
well maybe not a chill
but a heartbeat pause:
who dunnit?
because blood must be involved
to make those apples redder.
Then ducks and a rock
that didn't get redder . . .
You don't know what I'm talking about
unless you know this poem by Kenneth Patchen.
When I looked at it again not too far back
it didn't have the power
it had when I first read it
at seventeen
or heard him read it, rather,
on a record, but it's enough
that once it did have power,
and I am redder for what happened there.

How Long

i. m. Loren̦o Thomas

How long do you want to go on being the person you think you are?
How Long, a city in China

The nouns come toward you
"Knee how," they say
  To the cluster of synonyms also approaching
        . . . has that evening train been gone?
How long, how long, baby, how long?

Let me know
if you ever change your mind
about leaving, leaving me behind
or at least tell yourself
before you find yourself on that train
winding its way through the mountains of How Much Province

The ten thousand yellow leaves of the ginkgo tree
kerplumfed onto the sidewalk on East 12th Street,
a deep-pile carpet of them on the roof of the parked car
proving that Nature does have a sense of humor,
though if a sense of humor falls in the woods
and there is no one there to hear it . . .

for everyone has clustered alongside the railroad track
for the arrival of night and its shooting stars with trails like pigtails

I am among them and I know this track is mine
though it does not belong to me

Nothing belongs to me

for at this moment the boxes are being stacked
to make way for you to move through them,
reading their labels: family photos, Pick-Up Stix, miscellaneous

and the song of the porcelain, the celadon, and Delft itself
vibrating How long, how long
will this baby take to depart?

But I don't want to think about the past
I want to *be* the past,
with everything I've ever known and done
spread out on a two-dimensional plane
erected vertically and moving through the space I occupy on Earth

There is a lot more room left in me
though everyone I've ever known who's died is there
My mother my father say hello
to Ted and Joe and laugh with them
though Joe knows they are crying too
and that Ted is crying
and it sounds like laughter

They do this to console me
and I let them do it, to console them

What? I didn't hear you
or rather I heard you
but I couldn't make out what you said

The phone lay in its cradle
pretending to be asleep
and the blinking light made you think
that it was dreaming and that
there was someone you were supposed to call—
or were they supposed to call you?

Supposed. What does that mean.

It means no more than the contours of the landscape
that is as beautiful as the contours in John Ashbery's poetry
but it doesn't mean anything
unless you turn your mind on its side
and let it lie there
inert, and from this inertia
will arise a wing, the white wing
of a bird that has no anything else,
only this one wing
that folds and unfolds itself
like the magnetic field it rises above
in wave after wave after wave.

Then it's back to basics:
If you bone or debone a chicken

it comes out the same,
if you dust a cake with sugar
you add something
but if you dust your house you take away.
Oh to be a rock or a stone or even a pebble!
Momentarily,
for there is much that is unattractive about being a rock.
For one thing, I wouldn't be able
to finish this poem, I would sit here petrified
until they carted me away
to a park to serve as ornamental sculpture,
if I were lucky.

Now that you are convinced of something
that you already believed, the wallpaper becomes a fact
in the home of Anne and Fairfield Porter,
in the upstairs hallway and the bedroom
where Jimmy stayed, the wallpaper that here and there
was curling off the wall so Joe could tear it off
and glue it to a big white sheet of paper.
There is no other wallpaper
I would ever want.
Now the wallpaper goes away,
back on the wall in 1969
where I stood and gazed at it for a long time
and then went downstairs
to add coal to Fairfield's stove,
the big Aga he had shipped all the way from Sweden

because he was very determined to have it.
All day its warmth rose up to the second floor
and caressed the wallpaper.

Do you mind my going on like this?
You want something else, right?
Perhaps you want what you think poetry should give you,
but poetry doesn't give anyone anything,
it simply puts the syllables on the table
and lets you rearrange them in your head,
which you can do unless your head is a square
the size of the tabletop.
So why don't you lift your head off the table
and go lie down somewhere
more comfortable
and not worry about anything,
including the list of things to worry about
that you keep revising in your head,
for there is a slot through which that list
can slip and float down like a baby in a rocking crib,
down to a comfy dreamland
and be transformed into a list of gods whose jokes are wonderful.

But when the alarm goes off
the jokes don't seem funny
now that something is missing from them—
but what? (You weren't even asleep.)
It's not something you feel you're going to remember,

it's not as if you can go down the alphabet
until you get to a letter that has a special hum
because it's the first letter of the name
you can't quite recall,
it's not as if you can look just to the side of where
you think a dim star is and thereby have it magically appear.
The glow is gone,
and knowing it comes back sometimes
is little consolation.
But I'll take it
and go not to a deserted island
but to the factory where they make the bottles
that are washed ashore with a message inside,
and though the message has been blurred by water stains
it's a message, like the poetry in Valéry's saying
that poetry is something written by someone other than the poet
to someone other than the reader.
To you, Paul Valéry, *chapeau,*
though in some of your works no *chapeau,*
for in them it is not a bottle but a test tube
one finds one's finger stuck in.

•

What do you want to do with your life?
is a question asked of a young person
but slightly modified for an older one:
What do you want to do with the *rest* of your life?

Having control is an illusion we like to be fooled by:
the pinball machine of experience has bounced us
off one thing and onto another bing bing bing!
Life might be like a pinball machine
but it isn't one, and the trouble is
that you might be like a person
and you *are* one, as if in reverie,
but then it all seems crambe.

And so Sir Thomas Browne walks in
with an insane look on his face, he is searching
for examples of the number 5, do you
have any new ones for him? If not
please step aside, and out he goes
into the garden, eyes locked
onto the vegetation, the afternoon light
on the back of his coat.

You're relieved he didn't stay long.

For God's sake
here he comes again.
Lock the door!
But he performs osmosis
and becomes the door and then
the room and then you!
And you go about the house
looking for examples of the number 5

and you don't know why or where
it will all lead to.

But I do.
Who said that?
I did.
Why did you say that?
I didn't.
You didn't what? I heard you!
You mean you hurt me.
No, I . . . I see
there's no point in talking to *you*.

And there wasn't
for there was no one there,
only the residue of an idea
that lasted a few moments,
like the history of Bulgaria
or the rattling of bamboo trees in the wind
or the Millennium Hotel in Minneapolis.

The water lilies float on the surface of the water
unaware that they are being depicted
by brushstrokes

"I love to be beside your side
beside the sea, beside the seaside
by the beautiful sea!"

we sang
underwater glub glub
as the propeller turned to face us
and we fled
because Hitler was the propeller

and he was unsanitary

So Père Noël took a bath
whose bubbles rose up around his beard
and tickled his fancy
enough to keep him ho-ho-hoing throughout the holiday season,
for he was in denial
about his powerlessness
in the face of Hitler

Hitler kept a special area on his face
for the powerlessness of Santa Claus,
he wore it like a merit badge
among the many others that covered his face
so that no one could see what he really looked like,
the way Santa Claus used his beard to hide
the deep sadness he felt for all humanity,
for if he arrived on their rooftops weeping and wailing
it would not do,
it would not do to bring the children
model replicas of Auschwitz
or dolls in the form of the Butcher of Buchenwald
or even of himself with downcast eye and ashen brow.

The doctor comes in and says, "What seems to be the trouble?"
for the twenty-fifth time today
but you are only once today
so you say, "There's a pain in my chest it's been there for three days it
  started on Sunday night right after dinner,"
but the doctor is thinking about the dinner he is having tonight with an
  incredibly attractive woman
He is more worried about her than he is about your symptom
In fact he isn't worried about you at all
though he might be worried about being sued by you
if he tells you to go home and take an aspirin and when you do you die
But maybe you were going to die anyway
no matter what he said or did
and the lawyer who eagerly took the case on behalf of your family
was hit by a car as he crossed the street toward the courthouse steps
and your entire family was killed in a plane crash
on their way to a Grief Management Center in Arizona
But none of this happens because the pain
was due to a strained muscle in your chest
and now you do remember that right after dinner
you tried to stop in mid-sneeze
Two hundred dollars for half a sneeze
is the going rate these days

The cost of living sticks a hose into your wallet
and vacuums out the money in a trice
and you are so grateful you aren't having heart surgery
that you don't even notice

until cold air drifts across the floor
like fog in a horror film,
the one you decided not to be in,
and now it pursues you
in the form of frozen air,
the evil brother of cool air
that filtered down out of the early summer evening
and told you that the world is kind,
that atoms rearrange themselves to make you feel better,
that the sun is departing only because it felt
you wanted to be alone for a while

It didn't say, "I will never rise again,
I will go far away and be a pinprick in the sky
among the billions of others, and you
will never know which I am
and I will never tell you."

And you will never answer back, "Sun,
I do not think you have that power:
only I do, and I will go away and be the sky."

Is that what is meant by "aesthetic distance"?

Say what?

It's as if the Panama Canal had been given aesthetic distance
by becoming a passageway in your brain

and you floated down it and came out
on the end that you started at!

Hunh?

I keep a ball of laughter inside that *Hunh.*

The Joke

When Jesus found himself
nailed to the cross,
crushed with despair,
crying out
"Why hast thou forsaken me?"
he enacted the story
of every person who suddenly realizes
not that he or she has been foresaken
but that there never was
a foresaker,
for the idea of immortality
that is the birthright of every human being
gradually vanishes
until it is gone
and we cry out.

Anniversary Waltz

I wake up on my forty-fifth wedding anniversary alone,
sky overcast, floor fan whirring quietly,
and I feel pretty good, considering.
Forty-five is hard to pin down, it doesn't
have the solid force of forty or fifty
though it does have the feeling of being
a nice round number that isn't round,
technically speaking. But who could be technical
on a day such as this? My wife
in New York is not technical ever.
I love her. What does that mean?
It means something that you, if you're young,
might be lucky enough to feel someday
though you, like me, won't know
what it is. You'll wake up and think
Now I know what he meant
by not knowing, and you'll feel good.

An Air for Sir John Suckling

The sun just went behind a cloud
and/or a cloud just went in front
It's a dance they do and the moon
joins in with the stars sometimes

That's up in the empyrean
where no one goes anymore
nor to sylvan dells
where sprightly maidens dwell

I used to think that life
with such a lissome maid
would be heaven and
it is! here in this sylvan dell
I look up from and see
a car of fire streak 'cross
the blue and dark green light
bathed in its own embrace

The Best Thing I Did

The best thing I did
for my mother
was to outlive her

for which I deserve
no credit

though it makes me glad
that she didn't have
to see me die

Like most people
(I suppose)
I feel I should
have done more
for her

Like what?
I wasn't such a bad son

I would have wanted
to have loved her as much
as she loved me
but I couldn't
I had a life a son of my own

a wife and my youth that kept going on
maybe too long

And now I love her more
and more

so that perhaps
when I die
our love will be the same

though I seriously doubt
my heart can ever be
as big as hers

Statue Man

Could I have the strength
to lift my stone fingers to wave at you,
cloud,
in the dark of night
when I know you are there
above my roof
as I lie in bed
looking at the ceiling?
Could I have the strength
of character to salute you
whom we think of
almost as a person,
though it's a wasted gesture,
a whimsy that serves no purpose
but its own?
Why yes, I could,
if I wanted, but a man
with fingers made of stone
can't want to do that
or anything else,
for the only desire he has
is the one sent to him
on invisible waves
that shake his insides
so hard he wants to laugh.

Snake Oil Song

Let me walk right up to you
in this square on a fine September morning
and tell you of this fine elixir
known only to the old grandees of Spain
and the great pashas of Turkey

The shadow of the Flatiron Building
falls across us like a slab in a cemetery
but this elixir is as powerful as a sledgehammer
and as potent as a potentate,
it'll grow a mustache on a turnip

No of course not sir I did not mean
to say that you are in any way a turnip
or even incapable of growing a mustache,
I was speaking hypothetically
even about the cemetery and the shadow

For lo though I walk through the valley
of the shadow of the Flatiron Building
I will fear no turnip nor will I flinch
before the onrush of each day's horror,
for I have in hand this fine elixir
known only to the old grandees of Spain

and of course the great pashas of Turkey.
But you are thinking I am trying to sell
a bottle here and there—to you, perhaps.
But no, the answer is no, never,
I'll not give up this fine elixir,

though you outstretch your hand and beg
I'll take a step away and then one more,
and as you start toward me I'll step two more
then run, and you will chase me down the street
that leads away from the Flatiron Building,

you will chase me night and day,
though my image fade and disappear,
for the bottle never disappears and the elixir
flashes brighter, as if made of laughter.

From Dante

for George Schneeman

I

Guido, I want you and Giorgio and me
To dig a ditch just by singing
And mess around in a boat, which at every wind
Goes flying o'er the sea to your wish and mine.
Bad Luck, laughing all the while,
Cannot throw big rocks at my feet, but
Ouch! it hurts always living by your talent,
To stand always inside a crescendo!
And the moonlight hits two mountains
Like the number 50 coming in for a landing
And shining with our great songs,
For I have a reason to love you always,
Each one in his ditch contented,
As I think we all soon will be.

II

From that lady I see a gentle shiver
Go through all the passing saints
And our almost springlike snow
Falls like daytime on a broad lake.
From her eyes a light shines out
Like a little squint of flames
And I grow red hot like a cherry
And look—now I'm an angel.
On the day you say hello
With a piano in your kind attitude
You'll stab us to the heart with virtue
And the sky'll open up like a soprano
And your gaze will come across the earth
With the closeness of wind.

III

One day Melancholy came back to me
And said, "I want to stay with you a while."
And it seemed she had brought along
Grief and Rage as company.
And I said, "Go away!"
And she fell upon me like a Greek
And raged in my great head,
Made me look at Love arriving
Dressed again in that black curtain
And on her head a little chapel
And certainly pure glass tears
That made me cry, "I too have one bad thought
That, sweet brother, kills our love and makes us die."

Snowman

I don't know what I thought
when I looked out the window
at age eighteen in my dorm room
the snow whirling around above 114th Street
in a hard, fast, and sometimes cruel New York
or later in Paris age what was it
twenty-three on the passage Rauch
which felt wonderfully like nowhere
to be so hidden in Paris and in layers and layers
in the drafty old atelier
and then looking down at that big white-topped thing
what is it it's an Alp!
though at seven I do recall waking up
and seeing the snow outside and thinking
snowman snowball sled
which my dad tied to the rear bumper of the car
and pulled me down the snow-quiet street it
was the kind of thing we did in those days
the car went slowly and my dad said
If I stop, just roll off you'll be alright

I'm still alright or alright enough sixty years later
as I stand in my apartment and watch
the snow fall out of the cold-colored sky
and down between the buildings that line East 13th Street

Nothing can hurt me today I'm warm
and I don't have to go to a job or anywhere else
I can fix a pot of jasmine tea
and have half a prune danish,
take the other half on a tray to my wife
in the bedroom where she's taking it easy
with telly and a cup of tea for her too
and suddenly I cry for you I wish you
were looking out your window on St. Mark's Place
so I could call you and say *Sono io*
and hear you laugh at our inside joke
and say *Ronnie!*

I just heard you say it through your ashes

The Japanese Garden

In 1958 or '59 when I was sixteen
I came up with the idea
of replacing my parents' backyard
with a Japanese garden—
this in a middle-class neighborhood
of Tulsa, Oklahoma.
I even showed a design to my mother,
who tried to imagine her smooth green lawn
replaced by rocks, gravel,
and, somehow, a stream.
Even before she said diplomatically
I'll show this to your daddy
I saw that the whole idea was unrealistic,
and I put out my hand for the drawing,
relieved to be denied.

But what if my parents had gone on
not only to put in the garden
but also to demolish our house
and replace it with a Japanese one,
donned kimonos and learned Japanese,
my dad strutting among the pines like a samurai,
mother on bended knees, head bowed?

The house stayed the same, the grass grew
and got mowed, I went away to college,
my parents divorced.

Now someone else lives there,
happy among the cherry blossoms that never fall.

The Song of René Descartes

René Descartes is seated
at his table. He writes
with a pen on a piece
of paper that is exactly
the same size as that
of the table. The candle
is melting. Descartes begins
to melt, but he stops:
he must stay human a little longer.
Now he puts down the pen.
He is tired. Being Descartes
is very tiring
in an evening of yes
or no or yes and no.

Drat

The waitress
at lunch today
could have been
in a 1940s movie,
an innocent,
cheerful, and open
young woman—ah,
girl!—with a smile
that brings back
a time
that probably
never existed.
Did people
really say *Drat?*
Or just characters
in films
and comic strips
who now
are as real
as real people.

The Hole in the Wall

Through the wall to my right,
behind the bookcase with some books
that I first read as an adolescent,
my grandson is sleeping—his afternoon nap,
the kind you take when you're two years old
and which I'd have taken myself
had I not had a cup of dark English tea.
Some day I hope that he will sit where I am now
and have a cup of tea and be thrilled
to think his grandpa built this room, this house,
and this poem—the poem for him,
and though I didn't know it then
the room and house as well.

And when he's old enough to do that
I won't know what he's become
unless I live to a ripe old age
(which maybe I will, who knows?)
and have my wits about me,
at least enough of them to see
what kind of man he is.
I hope he's good and kind
and nobody's fool
except a fool like me,
a fool for him.

The Red Pool

Oh dear here we are again in a pool of blood
below a heavenly board in a sky of thought,
not the way Andrew Marvell thought
but more the way that history leaned, i.e. sideways

I am bending over backwards
to dodge the ideas that graze my face
before I tuck and roll and hit
the surface in (not of) a cannonball

and the red explodes concussing up
and out in a fine spray, leaving a hole
in Andrew Marvell's conversation.
What was all the talk about?

Hull, perhaps, the casks of wine delivered there,
unloaded on the docks at eventide.

The Brick of Bach

Come ye joyful nations, rise
Join the triumph of the skies

Register upon register
of nations and nations of angels
seraphim cherubs all the gradations
of heavenly spirits dappled pink
that fade out into pure white light
and singing not through their mouths
but through their being there
clavier upon clavier stacked
and fanned up and out amidst
the architecture of heaven

Who would not want to be a brick
in this city made of music or a note
like the one that becomes two when *rise*
becomes *ri-ise* and *skies* become *ski-ies?*
Can a brick sing yes
if it is invisible
and they are winning, those bricks

So come ye joyful nations, rise
Join the bricks up in the skies
and have brickness so much

that you too are an angel
a visible one
though the other you
is a little above
invisible and singing
the exact same note as you

Flame Name

I saw my name in boldface type
lying on the ground among the orange and yellow leaves
I had placed there to simulate autumn,
but someone else had placed my name there
and set fire to its edges.
The effect was lovely.
This was not, by the way,
a dream. It was also not
something that really happened.
I made it up, so I could
set my name on fire
for a moment.

The Coat Hanger

Starting from the left but seen from the right I am
an open parenthesis just like a doctor
told me I would be if I didn't start standing up straight
and I didn't. Almost fifty years ago
we heard a recording of Lord Buckley doing his Naz routine
in which Jesus of Nazareth encounters a poor hunched-over man
and asks him why he's like that and the man replies
"Mah *frame's* bent, Naz!" and we curled up
in spasms of laughter, and later Ted
put it in his poems as if he too were hunched over
though he wasn't except at the typewriter
and he was sometimes bent out of shape
psychically. He developed, as we say, a "bent" for it,
the way Whitman developed a bent for standing up straight
in his poems and proclaiming openness and Mallarmé
opened up his way of saying things in "A Throw of the Dice"
and Pound opened up the page to bursts of history literature economics
and general whatever you want, Olson declaring that
the poem is a field of energy you can put anything in and Frank O'Hara
putting himself in that field that turned out to be his heart,
—"you can't plan on the heart, but
the better part of it, my poetry, is open"—and Kenneth in later life
writing in a private journal that he had decided not to think about death
but about "things that keep opening up," and Joe too
always wanting to be as open as possible.

81

It's hard to do because everything rushes toward you
and demands that you close up a little here, a little there,
so you can have for instance breakfast instead of floating off over a star
ringed with glory and an immortality that goes on for an instant.
That's why or partly why (because everything is "partly") I
when seen from the right am an open parenthesis,
though at this very moment I am closing slightly
because I came to and found myself alone in a room:
the open part of me had disappeared
and been replaced by a strategy. But I am smarter
than any strategy when I remember that I am,
that majesty can build from its own underground
and exultation rises like a train station in the mind of a boy,
a station built of straight lines and sunlight-dappled water,
though you are dragging your great trunk along the ground
trying to figure out if you are legless or an elephant
and the dust rises about you like a chorus of angels
come not to sing thee to thy rest but to giggle like curlicues
in the air around the head of a headless person,
for though the body is dead the head is alive inside itself,
even more alive than when it was connected to the body.
I don't care what it will say to me
if I allow its lips to move for I
am feeling somewhat bent this morning and in no mood
for ghoulishness or foolishness: the water in the stream
flows onto this page and now onto you.
What did Whitman say? "This is no book;
Who touches this touches a man." With him that was very

almost true. Me I am at an angle,

but when I stand up straight as the lines in that station,

I see, before the fog rolls in, the tracks that take us all across ourselves,

metaphorical fog thicker than real fog,

just as barking is thicker than a dog,

though the dog is clearing up too, like a sky

whose translucence is arriving as the metaphors depart

and I start the day as a man for the first time again.

The Great Wall of China

This morning I am striding among the Chinese
on their way to work or school I'm on my way to breakfast
They don't seem unhappy the streets are clean
and they're in black more than I am in New York City black
Everything is OK the way it is

The rain on the Great Wall today makes it look sad
not because rain is sad
but because it makes the Wall seem even more useless
The Wall that was built to keep people out
now brings people in
I was thinking this this morning in bed
happy to be imagining the Wall and my being there later today
a place I've wanted to be ever since the moment I learned it existed
But now Anne Waldman walks up and says *Ni hao*
bowing slightly at the waist with a smile
How does she go on being Anne Waldman?
The same way the Great Wall goes on going on
—the great bonus of life—
but look out I am becoming too grand not great
and I haven't even seen the Wall yet I have hit
a wall the wall of seeing my old friend in the street
so I walk along the top of her head the view
on one side is New York on the other is the thing
the incredibly big and old thing the thing

that is secretly smiling it is what we call China
a large vase that shatters and reassembles itself time and again
like a clock that goes tick and then tock

Chinese air in my lungs I am lighter than usual
and the wall even the little part of it I am standing on at Badaling
is suddenly heavier than it was because it is connected to my feet
those of a millipede rolling its 4,000-mile-long body
into the past and back, I am thrilled at Badaling I am thrilled
by the very sound of the word *Badaling* and what
is useless in my life has taken wing into the aether that protects
    the human race

Am I great yet? no I am smaller and smaller
and happier to be so, soon I will be only one chopstick tall
and though they say that the journey of a thousand li
begins with a single step what they don't say is
that the single step is a thousand li long and it is joyous
because you don't know what a li is and you don't care
for there are li everywhere and they're fine where they are

The Wall of course has nothing to say
It used to groan and growl but now it's like a very old man
you think is grumpy but no he's not
Perhaps at a certain age holiness slips in automatically
and says Just sit there and don't say anything it's alright
But what did I hear was it the holiness of the Wall veering into
    the distance?

Then I come back standing there atop it
and above me the clouds on their way to New York
one of them shaped like the Wall and I am on it too

Children's Story

Ronnie did not want to take a nap.
Why take a nap?
He wasn't sleepy.
It was the middle of the day!

The teacher said it was time to take a nap.
Look at the other boys and girls.
They are lying down to take their naps.

That's fine for them, thought Ronnie,
and he said, I ain't gonna take no goddamned nap.

The teacher looked funny.
He thought she was like a babysitter
but she was different.

With the palm of her hand
she gave him a little whack on his behind.
Now don't you talk like that, she said.
You behave and take your nap.

Ronnie began to cry
as he got down on the pallet
where little cowboys and Indians were playing.
He laid his head on the pallet and cried.

Then after a while he stopped crying
because he had fallen asleep.

Later he and the other children woke up.
They rolled up their pallets
and started to play a game with the teacher.
Then it was time for his mother to come
with the other mothers.

And there she was.
The teacher told her that Ronnie had said Goddamn.
He did? said his mother. Well.
You can't say that at school, she told him.
And they went home together.

RON PADGETT is a celebrated poet, translator, and memoirist. His poetry has been translated into fourteen languages and has appeared in *The Best American Poetry, Poetry 180, Postmodern American Poetry: A Norton Anthology,* and *The Oxford Book of American Poetry,* and on Garrison Keillor's *Writer's Almanac.* A guest on Keillor's *Prairie Home Companion,* Padgett is also a Chancellor of the Academy of American Poets and the winner of the Poetry Society of America's Shelley Memorial Award. Born in Tulsa, he lives in New York City and Vermont.

Visit his website at www.ronpadgett.com.

COLOPHON

How Long was designed at Coffee House Press, in the historic
Grain Belt Brewery's Bottling House near downtown Minneapolis.
The text is set in Fornier.

FUNDER ACKNOWLEDGMENT

Coffee House Press is an independent nonprofit literary publisher. Our books are made possible through the generous support of grants and gifts from many foundations, corporate giving programs, state and federal support, and through donations from individuals who believe in the transformational power of literature. Coffee House Press receives major operating support from the Bush Foundation, the McKnight Foundation, from Target, and from the Minnesota State Arts Board, through an appropriation from the Minnesota State Legislature and from the National Endowment for the Arts. Coffee House also receives support from: three anonymous donors; Allan Appel; Around Town Literary Media Guides; Bill Berkson; the James L. and Nancy J. Bildner Foundation; the Patrick and Aimee Butler Family Foundation; the Buuck Family Foundation; Dorsey & Whitney, LLP; Fredrikson & Byron, P.A.; Sally French; Jennifer Haugh; Anselm Hollo and Jane Dalrymple-Hollo; Jeffrey Hom; Stephen and Isabel Keating; the Kenneth Koch Literary Estate; the Lenfestey Family Foundation; Ethan J. Litman; Mary McDermid; Sjur Midness and Briar Andresen; the Rehael Fund of the Minneapolis Foundation; Deborah Reynolds; Schwegman, Lundberg, Woessner, P.A.; John Sjoberg; David Smith; Mary Strand and Tom Fraser; Jeffrey Sugerman; the Archie D. & Bertha H. Walker Foundation; Stu Wilson and Mel Barker; the Woessner Freeman Family Foundation in memory of David Hilton; and many other generous individual donors.

This activity is made possible
in part by a grant from the
Minnesota State Arts Board,
through an appropriation by the
Minnesota State Legislature
and a grant from the National
Endowment for the Arts.

NATIONAL
ENDOWMENT
FOR THE ARTS

MINNESOTA
STATE ARTS BOARD

TARGET®

To you and our many readers across the country,
we send our thanks for your continuing support.

Good books are brewing at coffeehousepress.org

www.ingramcontent.com/pod-product-compliance
Lightning Source LLC
Jackson TN
JSHW080854211224
75817JS00002B/30